A Month's Journey with the Merciful Jesus

A MONTH'S JOURNEY WITH THE MERCIFUL JESUS

By Allan F. Wright

CATHOLIC BOOK PUBLISHING CORP.
New Jersey

NIHIL OBSTAT: Fr. Philip-Michael F. Tangorra, S.T.L.
Censor Librorum

IMPRIMATUR: ✠ Most Rev. Arthur J. Serratelli, S.T.D., S.S.L., D.D.
Bishop of Paterson

June 23, 2016

The Nihil Obstat and Imprimatur are official declarations that a book or a pamphlet is free of doctrinal or moral error. No implication is contained therein that those who have granted the Nihil Obstat and Imprimatur agree with the contents, opinions or statements expressed.

(T-54)

ISBN 978-1-941243-52-7

77 West End Rd.
Totowa, NJ 07512
Printed in the U.S.A.
www.catholicbookpublishing.com

Contents

INTRODUCTION

In the New Testament, the word that is most often translated as "mercy" is *eleos*. It can be translated as loving kindness or tender compassion. This Greek word *eleos* comes from a root word signifying oil that is poured out. Thus, when the Church sings in her liturgy the Greek words *Kyrie, eleison* and *Christe, eleison,* she is praying that the merciful love of God will be poured out, like oil from above. In essence, *eleos* is God's love poured out upon His people.

In the Latin tradition, the primary word for mercy is *misericordia*, which means "miserable heart." Mercy can be described then as the state of having one's heart touched with pain for a person who is suffering and then doing something to alleviate that pain. Pope St. John Paul II wrote in *Dives in Misericordia:* "The Bible, Tradition, and the whole faith life of the People of God provide unique proof ... that mercy is the greatest of the attributes and perfections of God" (no. 13).

The word "mercy" describes an action more so than an attitude; it's active in nature as opposed to a passive feeling that one might have. Concrete actions of loving kindness to those in need constitute the mercy desired by God. We see this quality of mercy displayed on the pages of the Gospels both by Jesus and a few persons whose merciful actions Jesus affirms.

Pope Francis has made mercy a prominent theme of his pontificate and speaks about it often. During a weekly morning *Angelus* he stated: "Jesus' attitude is striking: we do not hear the words of scorn, we do not hear words of condemnation, but only words of love, of mercy, which are an invitation to conversion. 'Neither do I condemn you; go, and do not sin again.' Ah! Brothers and Sisters, God's face is the face of a merciful father who is always patient. Have you thought about God's patience, the patience He has with each one of us? That is His mercy. He always has patience, patience with us, He understands us, He waits for us, He does not tire of forgiving us if we are able to return to Him with a contrite heart. 'Great is God's mercy,' says the Psalm," *Angelus*, March 17, 2013.

This book will take you on a journey of mercy through the life of Jesus as found in the four Gospels. Each passage of Sacred Scripture, each short reflection and prayer are designed to have you experience more fully the mercy of God and, in turn, be an active participant in sharing that mercy with others.

Traditionally, the four Gospel writers have been represented by the following symbols:

St. Matthew, a divine man; St. Mark, a winged lion; St. Luke, a winged ox; and St. John, a rising eagle. These symbols are taken first from the Prophet Ezekiel in chapter one: "Their faces were like this: each of the four had a face of a man, but on the right side was the face of a lion, and on the left side the face of an ox, and finally each had the face of an eagle...."

In the Book of Revelation (4:7-8), we find a similar description to the one we read in Ezekiel: "The first creature resembled a lion; the second, an ox; the third had the face of a man; while the fourth looked like an eagle in flight. Each of the four living creatures had six wings and eyes all over, inside and out. Day and night, without pause, they sing: 'Holy, holy, holy, is the Lord God Almighty, He who was, and who is, and who is to come!'"

These four images in both the Old Testament and the New Testament prompted St. Irenaeus (140-202) to liken them to the four Gospel writers because of the content of their Gospels and their particular focus on Christ. In his treatise *"Adversus Haereses"* ("Against Heresies," XI), St. Irenaeus speculated, "'The first living creature was like a lion' symbolizing His effectual working, His leadership, and royal power; 'the second was like a calf,' signifying His sacrificial and sacerdotal order; but 'the third had, as it were, the face as of a man,' — an evident description of His advent as a human being; 'the fourth was like a flying eagle,' pointing out the gift of the Spirit hovering with His wings over the Church. And therefore, the Gospels are in accord with these things, among which Christ Jesus is seated."

Each of these ancient symbols which point conceivably to the Gospel writers can give us pause to reflect on the different faces of mercy as they come to us through the Word of God, through the Sacraments of the Church and in the providence of everyday life. Each introduction to the individual Gospels will have a brief summary of these ancient symbols as they relate to mercy.

Week 1

Praying with Matthew

Human Figure

The Gospel of Matthew begins with the genealogy of Jesus, His human ancestral line going back to Abraham. St. Matthew was writing to a Jewish audience where this information would have been valuable. Throughout the Gospel account we encounter the humanity of Jesus as He takes the initiative in actively reaching out to sinners and the wayward. Jesus confronts those who do not act with mercy, compassion, and justice, and makes His mission our own as He gives the Church the "Great Commission" at the very end of the Gospel.

The Great Commission which St. Matthew records, directs us to go and make disciples of all nations, to baptize them in the name of the Father and of the Son and of the Holy Spirit, and to teach them to obey everything Jesus has commanded. At the heart of Jesus' teaching, of course, is mercy, the mercy which comes from the heart of God the Father and the mercy that the Holy Spirit continues to stir within all who believe in Jesus.

The original witnesses to the life, death, and resurrection of Jesus attest to Jesus' mercy and as disciples, followed Jesus' way of love. The challenge for the Church today and for all who believe is to go and do likewise. Where and how do we accomplish this? It is accomplished every time we sacrifice our time for another, when we forgive generously from our heart, when we pray for each other and when, like Jesus, we give our lives to God.

Each person is afforded multiple opportunities each day to live out the Gospel in the providence of their daily life. These reflections taken from the Gospel of St. Matthew lead us to know the mind of Christ and put the mercy we have received from God into daily practice.

1 IN OUR FATHER'S FOOTSTEPS

(Matthew 5:7)

Blessed are the merciful, for they will obtain mercy.

There is a beautiful and pivotal scene in the play *Les Miserables* when Jean Valjean, an ex-convict, meets the Bishop of Digne who welcomes him into his home. It was the meeting with the Bishop who accepts him for who he is and gives him a helping hand regardless of his criminal past that transforms Valjean's life.

The Bishop did two things by treating Valjean this way. First, he was showing Valjean mercy, and second, he was treating him with compassion so that he could start a new life without being further suppressed by poverty and the law. As the Bishop himself phrases it, "It is your soul that I buy from you; I withdraw it from black thoughts and the spirit of perdition, and I give it to God." The Bishop's mercy did indeed have a very redeeming effect on Valjean for after this act of mercy he became a new man, started his own factory, and dedicated his life toward showing generosity and compassion toward all. What impact will the mercy you show toward others have in making God's Kingdom on Earth a reality?

Prayer. Lord God, so often my thoughts are of receiving mercy from You and I rarely give a thought about showing mercy toward others. Come to my aid so that I may be merciful in my thoughts, words, and actions, especially to those whom the world sees as undeserving. Amen.

2 PRAY FOR YOUR ENEMIES

(Matthew 5:44)

But I say to you: Love your enemies and pray for those who persecute you.

On May 13, 1981, Pope St. John Paul II was crossing St. Peter's Square in Vatican City when an attempt was made on his life. Mehmet Ali Ağca, who had escaped from a Turkish prison after receiving a life sentence for murdering a journalist fired four shots which struck the pontiff. In spite of severe blood loss, the pontiff survived, and asked for all Catholics to pray for Ağca, whom he had "sincerely forgiven." Pope St. John Paul II later visited his would-be assassin where they had a private conversation and emerged as friends.

The Pope stayed in touch with Ağca's family during the latter's incarceration, and in 2000 requested that he be pardoned. Ağca later converted to Christianity and was released in 2010.

People who are not Christians may not read the Bible but they do read Christians! What an awesome responsibility and privilege to bear the name of Christian and represent Jesus to the world, and what a beautiful example of mercy displayed to the world through the witness of St. John Paul II.

Prayer. Jesus, Lord of all, You not only spoke the words of mercy but gave us an example to follow through Your actions on earth. May we who bear the name "Christian" be as merciful, prayerful, and loving as You in all things toward all people.

3 TRUST THE MERCY OF OUR FATHER

(Matthew 6:26)

Gaze upon the birds in the sky. They do not sow or reap or store in barns, and yet your heavenly Father feeds them. Are you not of far greater value than they?

The mercy of Jesus is communicated in His actions, but He also reassures us of His mercy with His words which the Church has treasured, preserved, and handed on to subsequent generations. The use of ordinary, everyday objects which are familiar to all are used to communicate God's love and mercy for us. The technique that we often find in the teaching of Jesus calls us to compare one thing to another.

In this case, Jesus compares the value of birds, whose needs are provided for by God, to people, who are infinitely more valuable than birds. In God's mercy, He reassures us of His provision in all things because He knows the tendency we have to be anxious, to worry. Jesus calls us to fix our gaze not only on the birds of the air but ultimately on heaven, where our Father Who loves us provides for our needs.

Prayer. Jesus our hope, when trials and anxiety come upon us and overwhelm us, remind us to fix our gaze on You. May Your provision for the birds of the sky inspire us to trust You in all things, great and small. Be present to us through the ordinary things of life and remind us that You are in control of both Heaven and Earth and that we will never face danger alone. Amen.

4 AN INVITATION TO MY MERCY

(Matthew 11:28-30)

Come to me, all you who are weary and overburdened, and I will give you rest. Take my yoke upon you and learn from me, for I am meek and humble of heart, and you will find rest for your souls. For my yoke is easy and my burden is light.

God's mercy was revealed in an extraordinary way to Sister Faustina, the first Saint of the new millennium, when she was a young, uneducated nun in a convent of the Congregation of Sisters of Our Lady of Mercy in Poland during the 1930s. Due to her three years of simple education, the tasks she was assigned to were the humblest responsibilities in the convent, usually in the kitchen or garden. However, she received extraordinary messages from our Lord and He asked her to record these experiences, which she compiled into notebooks. These notebooks are known today as the *Diary of Saint Maria Faustina Kowalska*, and the words contained within are God's loving message of Divine Mercy.

In one message revealed to her, Jesus says; "I have opened my Heart as a living fountain of mercy. Let all souls draw life from it. Let them approach this sea of mercy with great trust. Whoever places his trust in My mercy will be filled with My divine peace at the hour of death."

Prayer. Abba, Father of Mercies, I give You my life and entrust everything into Your loving hands including my joys and sufferings. Allow me to enter into Your rest with the knowledge that You are in control and that You are always at my side. Amen.

5 JUDGED BY MERCY

(Matthew 25:35)

I was hungry and you gave me something to eat; I was thirsty and you gave me something to drink; I was a stranger and you welcomed me.

The Italian Renaissance master Michelangelo painted the fresco on the altar wall of the Sistine Chapel that is titled, *The Last Judgment*. The painting depicts the Second Coming of Christ and the eternal and final judgment by God of all humanity. It's one of the most visited works of art anywhere in the world and it can take hours to decipher the imagery and to allow the mastery of Michelangelo's work to permeate one's being.

Jesus didn't leave us artwork, but He did leave the early disciples to remember and record His words which also communicate with power the Last Judgment. In these words of judgment we also find mercy. When judgment comes the measure that will be used is not how much we know, what degrees in Theology we may have, but in how we responded to the poor, the abandoned, to the "least among us." Mercy can be displayed through many beautiful artistic expressions yet the best expression comes not on a canvas or Vatican Chapel wall but through actions of service toward others.

Prayer. Christ our King, draw us closely to You through Your Word, works of great beauty, goodness, and truth. While drawing our gaze to heaven let us never forget the hungry, the sick, the imprisoned, and the poor and marginalized who are so close to Your Sacred Heart. Remind us that in serving them, we are serving Jesus in the distressing disguise of the poor. Amen.

6 MERCY FOR THE LEAST AMONG US

(Matthew 25:40)

"Amen, I say to you, whatever you did for one of the least brethren of mine, you did for me."

Jesus identifies Himself with the "least brethren of mine." How different is that mind-set than what we ordinarily find in the world of business, politics, sports, and other pursuits. We are almost trained at birth to stand out from others, to rise above the rest and are told that our unique features will set us apart from the huddled masses. Yet Jesus identifies with the poor, the hungry and thirsty, those imprisoned, ill and naked.

In the Latin tradition, the primary word for mercy is *misericordia,* which means "miserable heart." Mercy allows one's heart to be touched with pain for a person who is suffering, but it is not just a feeling of pity, for mercy entails actions which alleviate that pain in the other.

Prayer. My Lord and My God, may the compassion I feel for others be expressed in heartfelt actions for those who are less fortunate. May I never forget that the eternal state of my soul at the last judgment will be determined by the extent of mercy I witness to others, especially the "least brethren of mine." Amen.

7 MERCY EXTENDED TO ALL

(Matthew 28:19-20)

Go, therefore, and make disciples of all nations, baptizing them in the name of the Father and the Son and the Holy Spirit, and teaching them to observe all that

I have commanded you. And behold, I am with you always, even to the end of the world.

Pope Francis remarked in his Easter message of 2013, "Let us be renewed by God's mercy, let us be loved by Jesus, let us enable the power of *his* love to transform our lives too; and let us become agents of this mercy, channels through which God can water the earth, protect all creation and make justice and peace flourish." How appropriate that the Pope calls us to be renewed by God's mercy in light of the Great Commission of Jesus.

The responsibility of the Church and her members is to keep alive the message of God's infinite mercy and love not through word alone, but through the living actions of mercy. It's not an easy task for it is a divine task, one that can't be accomplished on our efforts alone. Thanks be to God who has poured out His Holy Spirit upon us to empower us to bring the love of Christ and His mercy to the world.

Prayer. Come Holy Spirit, stir within our hearts and strengthen our will to carry out the Great Commission. Empower us with boldness to proclaim Your mercy and forgiveness. When opposition arises, may You transform our anger into grace and help us graciously extend the mercy we have received to others so the world may experience true peace. In Jesus' name we pray, Amen.

WEEK 2

PRAYING WITH MARK

The Roaring Lion

The Gospel writer St. Mark is depicted as a roaring Lion because when he presents Jesus we find no infancy stories or birth stories of our Lord but are immediately placed at the beginning of Jesus' public ministry. St. Mark boldly begins with an affirmation that this is the beginning of the good news about Jesus the Messiah, the Son of God. The symbol of a lion may also describe the voice of St. John the Baptist as one who was "crying out in the wilderness" upon hearing the Word of God as Isaiah prophesied. His voice is imagined to have sounded like that of a roaring lion.

As our study of mercy poured out in the Gospel of St. Mark will reveal, Jesus is courageous and fearless in revealing His mercy even in the face of an angry crowd who oppose Him. Jesus was resolved to please God and not seek the approval of men as He revealed the loving presence and mercy of God the Father. Time and time again in St. Mark's Gospel, Jesus takes time for those on the margins, the poor and unwanted of His day. The simple healing touch of Simon's mother-in-law without saying a word, the forgiveness and healing freely offered to a paralyzed man, and the cure of a leprous man are but a few of the acts of mercy we encounter in Mark's Jesus.

The challenge for many believers today of course is to be merciful as Jesus was merciful and to do it courageously! This courage is indeed 'supernatural' because it does not come naturally. We need the assistance of the Holy

Spirit to speak boldly and the encouragement from the Church that this is the way of Christ.

The witness that our Holy Father, Pope Francis, provides is a daily witness to the world of what "living mercy" looks like. May we imitate the generosity of Pope Francis as he imitates Christ.

8 MERCY ABOUNDS IN THE HOME

(Mark 1:29-30)

> *Immediately on leaving the synagogue, he went with James and John into the house of Simon and Andrew. Simon's mother-in-law was lying in bed, sick with a fever, and they informed Jesus at once about her. Jesus approached her, grasped her by the hand, and helped her up. Then the fever left her, and she began to serve them.*

Saint Padre Pio reminds us to: "Pray, hope and don't worry. Worry is useless. God is merciful and will hear your prayer." These words of a modern Saint fit perfectly with the actions of the Apostles when Simon's mother-in-law was ill with a fever. The actions of the Apostles reveal their trust and hope in the mercy of Jesus by going to Him and expressing the situation. Without saying a word Jesus responds with a healing touch. Without saying a word the woman responds beautifully by serving Jesus and others.

What a simple plan of action when we encounter a crisis or difficult situation. Pray, hope, and don't worry because when we make our requests known to God He is present and is already at work in revealing His mercy to us.

Prayer. God of Mercy, there are times when we are anxious and worry about so many things that life brings our way. May our sincere, heartfelt prayer touch Your Sacred Heart and bring an answer to our suffering in mind and body. When answers don't come on our schedule, remind us that even in Your silence, You are present and have a plan for everything that comes to us in life. Amen.

9 Radical Mercy

(Mark 2:5)

On perceiving their faith, Jesus said to the paralyzed man, "Son, your sins are forgiven."

In 1986, Steven McDonald was a young New York City Police Officer. While patrolling Central Park with his supervisor, they questioned three teenagers whom they suspected of stealing bicycles. One of the teenagers, a

15-year-old boy pulled a gun and shot Officer McDonald three times. Doctors were able to save his life, but the incident left him paralyzed and in need of a respirator to breathe.

At the time of this heartbreaking event, McDonald and his wife, Patty, had not yet reached their one-year anniversary and were expecting their first child. Steven and his wife loved each other through it all. In spite of everything that had happened, Steven decided that revenge was not the answer. Rather than hold a grudge, he forgave the boy who shot him. While Officer McDonald remained physically paralyzed he was set free from a vengeful and callous heart by his deliberate act of forgiveness.

In a similar way, Jesus deals with the bigger problem in the paralyzed man's life which is sin, for Jesus forgives him first. What follows this act of mercy is healing. How often do we need to follow this prescription in life? Forgiveness first, then healing can begin.

Prayer. Merciful Father, how often do I desire healing without ever considering Your call to forgive. If it is Your will, relieve me from my physical ailments, but only after I have forgiven others and in all humility asked to be forgiven for my own faults. Amen.

10 A TOUCH OF HIS GARMENT

(Mark 5:27-28)

Having heard about Jesus, she came up behind him in the crowd and touched his cloak, for she thought, "If I simply touch his clothing, I shall be made well."

Sometimes a little is enough. While it is often our desire to do great things for others and to surpass and exceed what has been done previously, we can get caught up in trying to outdo ourselves and be left with the feeling that what I did was not enough. Those same desires are often translated in our longing to please Jesus. We want to do great things for God, we hope to please Him with some great work of service. In the case of the woman with the hemorrhage we see that with Jesus, a little can be enough to activate His mercy.

In all honesty we are not perfect, our faith falters at times and more often than not we fail to live as Jesus calls us. However, the desire to please Him does in fact please Him and like the woman who reached out to touch the hem of His garment, a little faith can be enough. In the midst of our imperfections we can begin each day by reaching out to Jesus in prayer and asking His guiding touch on our lives as we seek to do God's Will.

Prayer. Loving Father, draw me close to Your Sacred Heart. Allow me a few minutes in Your presence each day contemplating Your love and mercy. May I have an eye for those who need my assistance and take time for them as You take time for me. Amen.

11 Mercy Extends to a Family

(Mark 5:41)

He took the child by the hand and said to her, "Talitha koum!" which means: "Little girl, I say to you, arise!"

The miracles of Jesus are indeed remarkable. The recipients and eyewitnesses of these miracles were forever changed by the healing words and touch of Jesus. We must remember that whenever Jesus reaches out and heals a person that there is a family involved as well. In the case of Jairus' daughter who had succumbed to death, we know that this girl had a mother and father who loved her and cared for her. No doubt there were other relatives, grandparents, aunts, uncles and cousins who knew and loved this little girl, too. The words and touch Jesus extends certainly does impact a family in a positive way.

It's worth reflecting on the people in our lives who have reached out to us and made a positive difference. Consider the "ripple effect" that your kind words or merciful actions can have on others and the gift that your life can be to the world.

Prayer. Most loving Father, through Jesus, You communicate Your great love for us. In reaching out to a child you restored a family and forever changed their lives. Help me to raise others up—be it through my words or actions—if it's only through a smile. Help me to start serving where I can. Amen.

12 Mercy Unbound

(Mark 5:18-20)

As Jesus was getting into the boat, the man who had been possessed with demons pleaded to be allowed to go with him. However, Jesus would not permit him to do so, and instead told him, "Go home to your own people and tell them what the Lord has done for you, and how he has had mercy on you." The man then departed and began to make known throughout the Decapolis what Jesus had done for him. And everyone was amazed.

Most classical music critics agree that Beethoven's Symphony 5, movement 1, is one of the most exquisite and brilliant pieces ever composed. In fact, after Beethoven premiered his masterpiece in December of 1808 at a concert at the Theater an der Wien in Vienna, critic E.T.A. Hoffmann described with vivacious language his experience; "How this wonderful composition, in a climax that climbs on and on, leads the listener imperiously forward into the spirit world of the infinite! No doubt the whole rushes like an ingenious rhapsody past many a man, but the soul of each thoughtful listener is assuredly stirred, deeply and intimately, by a feeling that is none other than that unutterable portentous longing, and until the final chord—indeed, even in the moments that follow it—he will be powerless to step out of that wondrous spirit realm where grief and joy embrace him in the form of sound."

Similar is the experience of one who has received the touch of Jesus' mercy. It compels the person to share it with others and to express it through any means available raising those around us up and out of their grief.

Prayer. Lord Jesus, may the mercy I have received from Your loving kindness be extended and expressed to everyone I encounter through word and deed and art and song and by any means which is at my disposal. Amen.

13 He Took the Cup

(Mark 14:24)

This is my blood of the covenant, which will be shed on behalf of many.

Immediately before the consecration of the bread and wine during Mass, as he begins the Eucharistic Prayer, the priest extends his hands and prays; "To you, therefore, most merciful Father, we make humble prayer and petition through Jesus Christ, your Son, our Lord." The Eucharist is the source and summit of Christian life. The God whom we worship and is revealed by Jesus is addressed as *merciful Father.* How beautiful that the attribute of God that we recall at each Eucharistic celebration is mercy.

For Catholics who have been invited to partake of this sacrificial meal with God we know that while we are unworthy to receive His Body and Blood, we are invited nonetheless. May our participation in this meal lead us to be merciful to those whom we encounter. Perhaps we believe they don't deserve our mercy but then again, God has freely given us His mercy which we don't deserve but receive as a gift.

Prayer. Father of all mercies, remind me that Your mercy comes to me as a gift which is to be handed on to others generously. May any desire for vengeance or retaliation on my part be transformed into a moment of grace for others, especially for those who don't know Your love and mercy. Amen.

14 SMALL THINGS DONE WITH GREAT LOVE

(Mark 12:42-44)

A poor widow also came and put in two copper coins, that is about a penny. Then he called his disciples to him and said, "Amen, I say to you, this poor widow has given more than all the other contributors to the treasury. For the others have all contributed out of their abundance, but she out of her poverty has given everything she possessed, all that she had to live on."

Jesus noticed the actions of one of the biblical characters least members, a poor widow. He immediately called over His disciples to inform these future leaders of the Church that this is what God is looking for. A teaching moment from the Lord directing His students to this unnamed woman's humble and total act of trust in God's providence. This is an active faith in God that Jesus praises and that was included in Mark's Gospel.

The eyes of Jesus were looking for faith and found it in one of the least expected places; in the actions of this woman. While we don't know her name, we do get a glimpse of her heart, a heart totally dependent and trusting in God's will for she held nothing back. How beautiful the heart that holds nothing back when it comes to serving God and others! Her charitable actions were not overlooked by Jesus and in fact were used as a lesson to the disciples concerning the faith that Jesus praises. May we be as vocal as Jesus in acknowledging God's mercy and the mercy of others which have been generously poured out at our feet. May we, like this un-named woman and Jesus Himself, hold nothing back when giving to God. And when we have the opportunity to show mercy to others allow us to give all and to trust in Your provision.

Prayer. Loving Father, may Your eyes catch me trusting in Your love and mercy in the providence of my everyday life. Whether I am praised publicly or not, I know that You are pleased when mercy is freely given. Amen.

Week 3

Praying with Luke

Ox

St. Luke is believed to be the author of the Gospel that bears his name as well as of the Acts of the Apostles. According to the ancient historian Eusebius, he was probably born in Antioch, Syria of a prosperous Greek family and was trained as a physician. His Gospel is considered the most poetic by many and he uses the best grammar and the most eloquent and correct Greek of the New Testament. He shows Jesus not as the Jewish Messiah, but as the world's Savior and Lord. He had a high regard for the dignity of women, and they played an important part in his writings.

The symbol of the winged Ox is associated with St. Luke because of the sacrificial emphasis Luke places on the life of Jesus. His Gospel begins in the Temple where the daily Jewish sacrifices were offered and Luke emphasizes the sacrificial aspect of Jesus' crucifixion and death at the end of his Gospel. The mercy of God is seen in the face of Jesus who offered Himself as the sacrifice for our sins. The death and punishment we deserve for our rebellion and sin against God was paid for by Jesus' sacrificial death on the Cross. Such is the mercy of God.

How do we respond to that love? The only acceptable response to love is...love. There will be opportunities in our own life to sacrifice ourselves for the lives of others. Perhaps not in physical martyrdom, but there are opportunities to die to ourselves and choose the way of Jesus. When we follow Jesus' example of a life lived for others we begin to experience the truth that when we die to self, we begin to live.

15 THE ANNUNCIATION

(Luke 1:28-38)

The angel came to her and said, "Hail, full of grace! The Lord is with you." But she was greatly troubled by his words and wondered in her heart what this salutation could mean. Then the angel said to her, "Do not be afraid, Mary, for you have found favor with God. Behold, you will conceive in your womb and bear a son, and you will name him Jesus."

Approximately four hundred years separate the last book of the Old Testament from the first book of the New Testament. While God is unpredictable, He is never unfaithful. His mercy towards His people is revealed in a small village, tucked away in the shadow of Jerusalem, through a humble Middle Eastern woman named Mary.

Mary's "Yes" to God set into motion the salvation of all mankind through her son, Jesus.

Mary cooperated in bringing God's mercy to us incarnate, "in the flesh." God is still seeking out people to make His love and mercy known to others. Do not be afraid to tell of God's mercy to others and to be mercy for others as well.

Prayer. Merciful Father, You chose Mary to be the "Ark of the New Covenant," and she made room for Jesus in her life. Help us to always say "Yes" to Your will like Mary did and trust in Your mercy every step of the way. Amen.

16 THE MAGNIFICAT

(Luke 1:46-50)

And Mary said: "My soul proclaims the greatness of the Lord and my spirit rejoices in God my Savior. For he has looked with favor on the lowliness of his servant; henceforth all generations will call me blessed. The Mighty One has done great things for me, and holy is his name. His mercy is shown from age to age to those who fear him."

Mary is the preeminent evangelist for she boldly proclaims what God has done for and through her. She does not focus on herself but rather on what God has done through her. God has shown the strength of his arm, He has routed those who are arrogant, He has brought down the mighty and He has filled the hungry with good things. These are among Mary's list recalling the saving actions of God.

The first item on Mary's list is the mercy of God which is shown from age to age. The mercy of God is not an abstract idea or a new philosophy but revealed in a person, God's Son, Jesus Christ. He was sent for you and me that we may encounter God's mercy personally.

Prayer. Heavenly Father, thank You for the great mercy and love You have shown throughout Salvation History. From the first chapters of Genesis, Your mercy is revealed in Your provision for man and woman even when they disobeyed You. May we model that same mercy to those who may not know of Your love and may we, united with our Blessed Mother, speak of Your salvation to all. Amen.

17 MERCY IN THE MANGER

(Luke 2:7)

She wrapped him in swaddling clothes and laid him in a manger, because there was no room for them in the inn.

Most people who cast their gaze upon the Nativity scene during the Advent season and at Christmas have their eyes drawn towards the child in the manger. We are sure to find the donkey and the oxen as well as a few Angels surrounding Mary and Joseph as they behold their newborn son. The manger is a place of feeding and nourishment.

The mercy of God is revealed in the humility of Jesus Who comes to us as an infant born in an obscure village and not from a prominent city. It is here where we first encounter God in the flesh as He lays vulnerable to the world. He is approachable and accessible to the wealthy foreigners, the Wise Men, and equally accessible to the lowly shepherds who are called to "come and see." All people, young and old, rich or poor, from every nation and tongue are invited to encounter God's mercy in Jesus.

Prayer. Merciful Father, kings and royalty build walls, fences, and trenches to keep others out, yet You come to us as a vulnerable child, open to all. May others encounter that same humility and mercy in all who bear the name Christian. Allow us to build bridges and pathways to You through witness and dialogue so all people can experience Your mercy. Amen.

18 A BANQUET OF MERCY

(Luke 14:22-23)

Shortly afterward, the servant told him, "Sir, your orders have been carried out, and some room is still available." Then the master said to the servant, "Go out to the open roads and along the hedgerows and compel people to come, so that my house may be filled."

The mercy of God knows no bounds! Those who refuse the invitation to His love and forgiveness have only themselves to blame. Pope Francis reminds us that, "God's patience has to call forth in us the courage to return to Him, however many mistakes and sins there may be in our life.... It is there, in the wounds of Jesus, that we are truly secure; there we encounter the boundless love of His heart." This 'boundless love' is well expressed in the Parable of the Great Banquet where the invitation to dine with the Master is not only extended to all including the poor, crippled, blind and lame, but they must be compelled because the offer is so extraordinary.

When we do encounter Jesus' mercy and accept His invitation we are overwhelmed with love. God's love, like all love, demands a response. No one who has ever responded to God's love has been found wanting for His love is enough.

Prayer. Lord God, I am grateful for Your constant invitation to relationship with You through Your Son Jesus Christ. May I never be closed off or look down upon others whom You love as well. Use me to extend Your invitation of mercy to everyone who does not know You so that the banquet in heaven may be full. Amen.

19 WHY SO ANGRY?

(Luke 4:18-19)

> *The Spirit of the Lord is upon me, because he has anointed me to bring the good news to the poor. He has sent me to proclaim release to prisoners and recovery of sight to the blind, to let the oppressed go free, and to proclaim the year of the Lord's favor.*

In this familiar passage in which Jesus inaugurates His public ministry we read of 'good news,' 'release of prisoners' and 'recovery of sight to the blind' as well as a year of the 'Lord's favor' or a 'jubilee year.' Immediately afterwards we read of the hostility of the crowd who seek to throw Jesus off a cliff. Why the hostility? Why the anger? What did Jesus do that strikes such a chord of discontent among the town's people?

Jesus omits the verses from Isaiah concerning strangers and foreigners being Israel's servants. For those nations who did harm to Israel and for people who had no regard for God there is mercy. An oppressed people desire vengeance, yet Jesus speaks of mercy. Opportunities for revenge will present themselves to us as well so we should remember that vengeance is God's and through the power of the Holy Spirit we can allow our anger to be transformed into mercy.

Prayer. Father of Mercy, pour out Your Spirit upon us so we may transform our anger into mercy. Use us as ministers of mercy in the providence of our daily lives. Open our ears and eyes, pierce our hearts, and strengthen our resolve to proclaim Your mercy and love. Amen.

20 MERCY DISPENSED

(Luke 10:33-34)

But a Samaritan who was traveling along that road came upon him, and when he saw him he was moved with compassion. He went up to him and bandaged his wounds after having poured oil and wine on them. Then he brought him upon his own animal to an inn and looked after him.

In the parable of the Good Samaritan, before any words are spoken, we observe the mercy of the Samaritan, a foreigner, being poured out on the wounds of an injured person. No identity is revealed concerning the injured man for he is stripped and unable to communicate, yet that doesn't prevent the Samaritan from offering aid and comfort. We observe that the priest went to the other side, the Levite went to the place, and the Samaritan went to the person.

What opportunities do you have that may be right in front of you to offer healing and mercy? If not through concrete actions then through words which can act as a salve to the soul and uplift the human spirit.

Prayer. God of Mercy, open my eyes so that I may respond to the sufferings of others. Open my ears to the sound of their cry. Open my heart so that those I encounter along life's way will leave my presence knowing that they are loved and precious in the sight of God. Amen.

21 A Merciful Meal and a Converted Heart

(Luke 19:5-6)

When he reached that spot, Jesus looked up and said to him, "Zacchaeus, hurry and come down, for I must stay at your house today." Zacchaeus came down quickly and welcomed him joyfully.

Many consider Rodgers and Hammerstein's play, *Carousel*, the best musical of the 20th Century. It spans both heaven and earth in its consideration of human fragility, resilience, and the power of forgiveness. The main character Billy, is allowed to spend one day on earth with his wife and daughter fifteen years after his death. In a nutshell, Billy instills in his wife and child a sense of hope and self-worth which speaks to the power of love's transcendence.

Jesus too, instilled a sense of hope and dignity to a publicly known and despised sinner named Zacchaeus. It was through Jesus' public demonstration of unexpected mercy that Zacchaeus' heart was forever changed. Mercy still has the power to convert even the hardest of hearts and to restore hope in even those whom we may consider farthest from God.

Prayer. Lord God, may I lead with mercy and love and never with condemnation of those I meet. May I never condemn those who are far from You, and may any harsh or uncharitable words I hear about others be washed away in a flood of Your mercy. Amen.

WEEK 4

PRAYING WITH JOHN

Eagle

The Gospel of St. John is radically different in style than the three synoptic Gospels. When reading the poetic prologue in chapter one the reader quickly realizes that this is no ordinary book. While Matthew, Mark, and Luke draw from their personal experiences and eyewitness accounts concerning the events that took place with Jesus, St. John provides us with a view from above. For this reason St. John is associated with the symbol of the eagle.

The eagle was believed to be the only creature who could gaze directly at the sun and not blink. So too, does St. John gaze at Jesus unapologetically and identify Him as God in the flesh, the Word of God who dwelt among us. St. John was one of the first Apostles called to follow Christ so he was present at the beginning of Jesus' public ministry, and he was also the only Apostle who was present at the Cross while the others abandoned Him out of fear.

It is this view from above that allows us to glimpse the mercy of God poured out in Christ who is in control in every situation. It is the mercy from Christ who goes to those on the margins; mercy from Christ who changes water into wine; mercy from Christ who washes His disciple's feet. It is the mercy from Christ that transforms the bread and wine into His very Body and Blood. May the mercy we encounter and experience in Christ so overwhelm us that we allow His mercy to be poured out through us as well.

22 THE LAMB OF GOD

(John 1:29)

The next day John saw Jesus coming toward him, and he said, "Behold, the Lamb of God, who takes away the sin of the world."

The earliest known liturgical use of the phrase, "Lamb of God, you take away the sins of the world: have mercy on us" and its repetition, is to be found in the well-known hymn of praise *Gloria in Excelsis Deo*, which Pope Symmachus (498-514 AD) made obligatory throughout Christendom at all Masses celebrated by bishops. According to the Traditional rubrics, the breast was struck at the words "have mercy on us" *(miserere nobis)* and "grant us peace" *(dona nobis pacem)*.

During the Communion Rite in the Roman Catholic Liturgy, after the sign of peace, faithful Catholics once again join the long tradition of reciting those words, mindful of the mercy of God. God's love has indeed been incarnate, made flesh, in the person of Jesus but it doesn't end there. He awaits us, each and every one of us, offering Himself, body, blood, soul, and divinity in the Eucharist.

Prayer. Jesus, Lamb of God, have mercy on us who, while being unworthy of You, are nonetheless invited into Holy Communion with

You through the sacrifice of the Mass. May the mercy we receive in Your precious Body and Blood be made manifest through our merciful actions towards others, especially to those who don't know You. Amen.

23 GOD'S MERCY TAKES INITIATIVE

(John 5:5-6)

A man who was there had been an invalid for thirty-eight years. When Jesus saw him lying there and was aware that he had been ill for a long time, he said to him, "Do you want to get well?" The invalid answered him, "Sir, I have no one to put me into the pool when the water is stirred up. While I am still on my way, someone else steps into the pool ahead of me." Jesus said to him, "Rise! Take up your mat and walk!" Immediately, the man was cured, and he took up his mat and began to walk.

Archaeologists have discovered several snake figures carved into the walls after excavating the pool where Jesus healed a paralyzed man. There is some evidence that the expanse also accommodated an 'Asclepeion', a pool dedicated to the Greek god of healing, Asclepius. Until the 19th century, there was no evidence outside of John's Gospel for the existence of this pool so academics argued that the Gospel was written by someone without first-hand knowledge of the city of Jerusalem. In their minds the pool had only a symbolic, rather than historical, significance. Yet, archaeologists and tourists alike can confirm that this ancient pool exists and was operating even years before the birth of Jesus.

One thing that we know today that the ancients were perhaps unaware of is the underground system of small water channels and springs which brought water to this pool. This is where the invalids would wait in anticipation of the "miraculous" stirring of water in the hope of being made whole by the Greek "god" Asclepius. The belief was that if they were the first one in the "stirring waters," agitated by the unseen springs, they would be healed of their ailment and would then regain access to their family and society and they would be whole.

It is possible then that the blind, lame, and paralyzed people who were gathered around this pool were not hoping for the God of Israel to heal them, but rather the mythical "god" Asclepius. The tension in the passage can be voiced as such: Who do you believe can heal you? The "god" Asclepius, or Jesus who claims to be God? In a beautiful act of mercy, Jesus takes the initiative and commands the man to rise, pick up his mat and walk. Jesus is still providing healing and wholeness to those whom He calls and to those who reach out and place their trust in Him.

Prayer. Father of mercy, may our hope be always focused on Your loving care for us. Guide us away from false hope in things other than Yourself. Amen.

24 FEASTING ON THE MERCY OF GOD

(John 6:35)

> *Jesus answered them, "I am the bread of life. Whoever comes to me will never be hungry, and whoever believes in me will never be thirsty."*

Many of us have had the experience of being welcomed in a home where food is the major way that love is communicated. Whether it's an Italian grandmother or Middle Eastern relative, food takes center stage. To refuse the food would be an insult to the host and a great affront to the family so the plate gets stacked high and our stomachs are filled to capacity.

In the Middle East where Jesus lived, table fellowship was and is still a way to define family and acceptance. To be welcomed around the table to share a meal meant that you were part of the family. Jesus was criticized and disparaged by His accusers for eating with and sharing meals with those whom they considered outcasts and sinners yet this never stopped Him from doing so.

Jesus' love and mercy is so great that He desires all people to come to Him, to be fed by Him and nourished by His word and through the Eucharist, His very Body and Blood.

Prayer. Jesus our hope, You never cease loving us and offering Yourself to us under the appearance of bread and wine. May we receive You with joyful hearts and may the mercy we encounter in You be poured out to others whom we meet on life's journey no matter how far from You they may be. Amen.

25 SEEING GOD'S LOVE

(John 9:1-7)

As Jesus walked along, he saw a man who had been blind from birth. His disciples asked him, "Rabbi, who sinned, this man or his parents, that he was born blind?" Jesus answered, "Neither this man nor his parents sinned; but it happened so that the works of God might be revealed in him. We must do the works of him who sent me while it is still day. Night is coming when no one can work. While I am in the world, I am the light of the world." When he had said this, he spat on the ground, made a paste with the saliva, and smeared the paste on the eyes of the blind man. Then he said to him, "Go and wash in the Pool of Siloam" (The name means "Sent"). So the man went forth and washed, and he returned seeing.

According to the World Health Organization, in the year 2012 there were 285 million people who were visually impaired of which 246 million had low vision and 39 million were blind. Today we have far more remedies and resources for those who are visually impaired than were available in Jesus' day yet blindness remains a severe loss. Jesus, when encountering those who were blind, offers healing and restoration of sight. Yet Jesus didn't magically cure everyone who was or is blind worldwide but assisted only those whom God brought His way.

Often we desire to do great things for God and providing comfort and healing is certainly part of the ministry of the Church. Perhaps we can reflect on Jesus' healing and helping those whom He encountered in the providence of His daily life. Who do you encounter on a regular basis at home, school, or in the work-place? Who are those you meet quite expectantly each day? Could God be placing them in your life as an opportunity to help them, to reveal God's love and mercy to?

Prayer. God our Father, open our eyes to those whom I meet and pass every day that I might encounter Christ in them. Prepare my heart and mind to offer them a word of encouragement and hope so that they would see Your love and experience Your mercy. Amen.

26 GAVE HIS ONLY SON

(John 3:16)

> *For God so loved the world that he gave his only Son, so that everyone who believes in him may not perish but may attain eternal life.*

There are well over fourteen thousand songs with the word love in the title. It seems that each new generation longs to know what this word love means and so we sing about love in all of its many forms and expressions because love is what the human heart desires most. In order to know what love is we must first encounter the source of all love which is God.

God, in His mercy, has revealed that love to us in the person of His son, Jesus Christ.

What a gift it is to be able to know what true, authentic, and life-giving love is. One Hebrew word for love is *ahava*, which has at its root the word *give*. How beautiful that the words *love* and give are so closely united and that God's love, like all love, is not withheld but is freely given and revealed in the person of Jesus.

Prayer. Lord God, may my love for You be put into action and given freely to others who are themselves looking for love. May my active belief be a source of strength for those who are searching for meaning and purpose in life. As You freely gave Your Son to us, may I give myself in service to others. Amen.

27 MERCY PUBLICLY ON DISPLAY

(John 8:11)

"Neither do I condemn you," Jesus said. "Go on your way and sin no more."

In one of the most dramatic scenes in the Gospel, a nameless woman, caught in the act of adultery, is dragged out publicly and thrown before Jesus. She knows the penalty for such behavior as do the Pharisees who brought her there. Jesus, too, is fully aware of what the law prescribes for such a "sinner."

While many speculate about what was written on the ground by the finger of Christ, I'm convinced that it was the law that stated the penalty for such an offense. The statement Jesus then posed to her accusers is one that continues to challenge those who hear it today, "Let anyone among you who is without sin be the first to throw a stone at her." Yes, the law prescribes death but mercy is on display through the words and actions of Jesus who shows a costly demonstration of love to a sinful—yet forgiven—woman. There is power in holding a weapon but Jesus shows us a better way. The way of mercy unites us with the power of God.

Prayer. My Lord and my God, forgive me for those times when I am self-righteous and would choose to condemn rather than to forgive. Send Your Holy Spirit to enkindle Your fire of love within me and to extend Your mercy to those who most need it. Amen.

28 A Compassionate and Merciful Witness

(John 13:5, 15)

Then he poured water into a basin and began to wash his disciples' feet and to wipe them with the towel wrapped around his waist.... "I have given you an example. What I have done for you, you should also do."

The *St. Joseph Guide to the Catechism* reminds us that the Church in the New Testament is described as the "Body of Christ" and there are other images derived from "pastoral and agricultural life" such as; "sheepfold of God, tillage of God, even building of God or God's dwelling place among men."

Jesus provides another image of the Church when He washes His disciples' feet which is Church as servant. What a powerful witness Jesus provides by this humble action that is repeated symbolically each Holy Thursday. Such is the mercy of our God that Jesus, the poured mercy of God in flesh, pours out water to wash our feet. Words of mercy are indeed powerful. Merciful actions however are what resonate within the human soul.

Prayer. Loving Father, may the waters of baptism which were poured over me as a child remind me to be humble like Yourself and to be a foot washer in whatever situation I find myself. I offer all my work, even the most mundane and menial, into the loving hands of Your mercy. Amen.

More Mercy
Thoughts for Reflection

29 A Merciful Father with the Heart of a Mother

(Luke 15:20-21)

So he set out for his father's house. But while he was still a long way off, his father saw him and was filled with compassion. He ran to him, threw his arms around him, and kissed him. Then the son said to him, "Father, I have sinned against heaven and against you. I am no longer worthy to be called your son."

There is a touching verse written by popular composer Don Henley that is worth contemplating in light of the words and actions of the Prodigal Son: "What are these voices outside love's open door, make us throw off our contentment and beg for something more?" The Prodigal Son squandered his inheritance but more significant and heart-wrenching is the fact that he squandered his relationship with his father. In the Middle Eastern culture in which Jesus told this story, the actions of the son would have merited death for the lad.

How beautiful is this father who transforms his anger into grace through running to his son in public view.

There is a Semitic proverb which says, "A man is known by his walk." This father disregards the slow, even paced, respectable walk of his contemporaries and runs to his son even before the son's confession escapes his lips. God is not like a father, He is like *this* father whose mercy and love for his son is on public display.

Prayer. Father of Mercies, Your love for us was on public display on the Cross, visible for all to see. Remind us of Your mercy and that there is no sin we can imagine that is greater than Your mercy. Send forth Your Holy Spirit to be at our side and call to mind Your mercy, forgiveness, and unconditional love at every turn of our life. Amen.

30 THE LAST SUPPER

(Luke 22:19)

> *Then he took bread, and after giving thanks he broke it and gave it to them, saying, "This is my body, which will be given for you. Do this in memory of me."*

Throughout the Old Testament we observe a number of sacrificial or covenant meals with

God. The most significant covenant meal was, of course, the Passover meal in which an unblemished lamb was sacrificed and consumed. Eating with other people was a significant event in ancient days, for only parties who were at peace could dine together. God takes the initiative to remind His people of the covenant He has made with them and of His never-ending faithfulness even when His people are unfaithful.

Jesus Himself is our Passover, He is our sacrificial lamb in which we have peace with God. During the Order of the Mass the priest says: "May the receiving of your Body and Blood, Lord Jesus Christ, not bring me to judgment or condemnation, but through Your loving mercy be for me protection in mind and body and a healing remedy." God's mercy is extended to all at every celebration of the Eucharist and His invitation to be at peace with Him is always awaiting a reply.

Prayer. Lord Jesus Christ, Lamb of God, through Your obedience to the Father You took away the sin of the world, thus creating a way for us to be at peace with God. May we gather around the altar where Your love and mercy are on display and through our participation in this heavenly banquet may we bring Your peace and mercy to others. Amen.

31 Mercy from the Cross

(Luke 23:32-34)

There were also two others, both criminals, who were led away to be executed with him. When they came to the place called The Skull, they crucified Jesus there along with the two criminals, one on his right and the other on his left. Then Jesus said, "Father, forgive them, for they do not know what they are doing."

In the culture where Jesus was raised the two driving forces which shaped human behavior were honor and shame. Therefore any 'sinful' behavior had to be either hidden or avenged. The way of vengeance and revenge is as old as Cain and Abel and continues to be the approach in many parts of the world. Jesus, however, shows us another way, the way of forgiveness. The anger and pain He experienced was transformed into mercy as expressed in His forgiveness of those who nailed Him to the Cross.

The forgiveness Jesus expresses on the Cross to His executioners was not a 'one time' event but rather the culmination of a lifetime spent forgiving others. To forgive and to ask forgiveness is not easy. Yet we find that when we forgive we follow in the footsteps of Jesus and participate in His divine life.

Prayer. Merciful Father, the example You give us is not easy but it is the way to joy and peace. May Your Holy Spirit enliven our hearts to have the grace to forgive others even when they act out of vengeance and ignorance. May we extend merciful forgiveness to others as we have received it from You. Amen.

APPENDIX

ROSARY OF THE DIVINE MERCY

The Rosary of the Divine Mercy is recited on an ordinary rosary. We can say it preferably for the great intentions of the Church and the world: the unity of Christians, the conversion of sinners, the return of a nation to God, peace among human beings, and the like.

ON THE SINGLE BEAD, SAY:

Holy Father, I offer You the Body and Blood, Soul and Divinity of Your Son Jesus in reparation for our sins and the sins of the whole world.

ON EACH OF THE TEN BEADS (DECADE), SAY:

By His sorrowful Passion, have pity on us and on the whole world.

AT THE END OF EACH DECADE, SAY:

Holy God, mighty God, eternal God, have mercy on us.

AT THE END OF THE ROSARY, SAY:

Blood and water that issued from the Heart of Jesus as the Source of mercy for us, I put my trust in You.

Spiritual Works of Mercy

1. To admonish the sinner (correct those who need it).
2. To instruct the ignorant (teach the ignorant).
3. To counsel the doubtful (give advice to those who need it).
4. To comfort the sorrowful (comfort those who suffer).
5. To bear wrongs patiently (be patient with others).
6. To forgive all injuries (forgive others who hurt you).
7. To pray for the living and the dead (pray for others).

Corporal Works of Mercy

1. To feed the hungry.
2. To give drink to the thirsty.
3. To clothe the naked.
4. To visit the imprisoned.
5. To shelter the homeless.
6. To visit the sick.
7. To bury the dead.